· I Want to Know™ ·

About PRAYER

Rick Osborne and K. Christie Bowler

ZondervanPublishingHouse

Grand Rapids, Michigan

A Division of HarperCollins Publishers

28

For Lightwave
Managing Editor: Elaine Osborne
Art Director: Terry Van Roon

The images used on page 5, 9, 10, 18, 19, 20, 21, 28 and 29 were obtained from ISMI's Master Photos Collection, 1895 Francisco Blvd. East, San Rafael, CA 94901-5506, USA.

Library of Congress Cataloging-in-Publication Data

Osborne, Rick, 1961– .
     Prayer / Rick Osborne and K. Christie Bowler.
          p.   cm.—(I want to know™)
     Summary: Discusses what prayer is, the importance of prayer in our lives, how to pray, and different types of prayer.
     ISBN 0–310–22091–2 (hardcover)
     1.   Prayer—Christianity—Juvenile literature.   [1. Prayer. 2. Christian life.] I. Bowler, K. Christie 1958– .
II. Title. III. Series: Osborne, Rick, 1961– .
I want to know™.
BV212.073   1998
248.3'2—dc21   98-11306
                                                      CIP
                                                      AC

This edition is printed on acid-free paper and meets the American National Standards Institute Z39.48 standard.

Published by Zonderkidz
The Children's Group of ZondervanPublishingHouse
Grand Rapids, Michigan 49530
www.zonderkidz.com
Zonderkidz is a trademark of The Zondervan Corporation

Printed in Mexico.
All rights reserved.

Building Christian faith in families

A Lightwave Production
P.O. Box 160 Maple Ridge
B.C., Canada V2X 7G1

99 00 /DR/ 5 4 3 2

Contents

4

Prayer Is Communication

It's Simple

Talking! Laughing! Singing! Whispering! SHOUTING! Telling secrets. Sharing problems. Chatting. What do these have in common? They're all ways we communicate. And they're all things we can do with God. When we do them with God, they're called *prayer!*

Prayer can be fun! It's simply communicating. Prayer is telling God what's on our hearts—what we feel, think, want, and need. And it's telling him what other people (our family, friends, neighbors, and strangers) need and want, too. It's like having a really good conversation with someone we can trust, and relax and be ourselves with.

Sound simple? It is. It's as simple as talking, laughing, singing, whispering, SHOUTING. . . .

The Big Silence

Imagine waking up one day to discover all sounds are sucked right out of the air and all writing erases itself! No communication! No asking for that special dessert.

No TV (aaagh!). No "I love you" or "Thanks." No asking for help. No songs or stories. No praise or correction. The airwaves are empty. Quiet, huh?

After a while it would feel lonely, too. Unless you learned sign language, no one would know what you're thinking or feeling, what worries you or makes you happy. In fact, no one would know much about you. And you wouldn't know much about them either. No relationship! No friendship!

This silence is what it's like between God and people who don't know him.

The Silence Ends

Once we get to know God, the silence is over! Ending it is pretty simple—we just become God's children (see page 25). Suddenly the communication airwaves between God

*The dove represents the Holy Spirit.
The Holy Spirit helps us to pray.*

all about prayer, and he sent the Holy Spirit to help us pray.

Are you ready to learn about this thing called prayer? Ready to start filling the airwaves between God and you? Dig in for guidelines, answers, information and fun! Here we go!

Kids Say

"God is my friend. . . . I ask him to help me remember how much he loves me." —*Timmy Gill, Florida*

"Kids can talk to God about anything. I do. If I'm feeling bad and don't feel I can tell anybody, I just talk to God about it. It helps me feel better, and he always helps me through things." —*Jacki Bliffen, Florida*

"Kids can pray every day. They can tell God they love him." —*Kristin Roker, Bahamas*

and us start humming! We can build a friendship with him—a Father-child kind of relationship—where the Father accepts us completely, spends time with us, and always listens to us. This Father wants to protect, guide, teach, and take care of us. He wants a great relationship with us, a relationship grown through communication—through prayer! Love—that's what it's all about.

Prayer fills the airwaves between us and our Father God.

But What About ...?

Sometimes prayer seems complicated. How do we talk to God when we can't see him? What should we pray about? How does God hear us? What's the right way to pray? Do we have to close our eyes? Does God always answer? There are as many questions as there are people.

God knew we would have questions, so he gave us the answers. He gave us his book, the Bible, to tell us

*God's book, the Bible,
teaches us about prayer.*

Prayer as Relationship

Family Language

Imagine two friends talking. Brad complains, "Dad never plays ball with me! He doesn't even care about what I like to do!"

Tyler asks, "Have you asked him to play ball with you?"

"Naw," Brad answers. "He wants to talk, but I'm not into that!"

Relationships are about loving and understanding each other and doing things together. But they're built by conversation. How will his dad know Brad wants to play ball if Brad never tells him?

It's the same with God and prayer. He wants us to talk to him. He knows everything, but he respects us and our choices. Getting to know God and growing with him isn't automatic—it happens through prayer. We tell God about our friends, how we're doing, what's going on in our lives . . . everything important to us. He loves to know. He loves us more than we can imagine. He wants the best life for us and knows how we'll get it. He'll train us in the skills we need and help us grow into fantastic people!

Since this all happens through prayer, that makes prayer pretty important. It's the foundation, the communication language of God's family.

Prayer Is . . .

Which of these things is not like the others: telephone, map, clothes, party, treehouse, father.

Father is the only person on the list. Father is whom we pray *to*. The others are what prayer is *like*.

Telephone: keeps us in touch with our friends, just as prayer connects us to God.

Map: shows landmarks, danger spots, and the best way to get places. Through prayer, God helps us to see where we're heading and to make the best choices to arrive there safely.

Clothes: cover us and protect us from cold. When we pray, God protects us and keeps us safe.

Party: celebration and fun. Prayer can be a great time of thanking God and celebrating the good things he's done. Enjoy it!

Treehouse: a private place to spend time with a good friend. Prayer is that special place where we spend time with God. We share our secret wishes and thoughts, and we ask God to share his. It's the place where we can really get to know God.

Why did our Father God give us prayer so we could get to know him? Because he loves us to pieces!

Made for Relationship with God

"A father is tender and kind to his children. In the same way, the Lord is tender and kind to those who have respect for him" (Psalm 103:13–14).

"I will be your Father. You will be my sons and daughters" (2 Corinthians 6:18).

"Because you are his children, God sent the Spirit of his Son into our hearts. . . . By his power we call God 'Abba.' Abba means Father" (Galatians 4:6).

"God chose us to belong to Christ before the world was created. . . . He loved us. So he decided long ago to adopt us as his children" (Ephesians 1:4–5).

"How great is the love the Father has given us so freely! Now we can be called children of God. And that's what we really are!" (1 John 3:1).

"Don't worry about anything. Instead, tell God about everything. Ask and pray. Give thanks to him" (Philippians 4:6).

Prayer Gone Bad

In the Beginning

Have you ever received a terrific gift? It works great! You enjoy it for a while. Then it breaks and just doesn't work the same anymore. That's what happened to prayer.

When God made the first people, prayer worked as it was designed to. Adam and Eve had a fantastic relationship with God. They knew they were his deeply loved children. They talked to him about anything. Nothing got in the way of their relationship with their Father.

The Big Mistake

Then Adam and Eve disobeyed God: *Sin!* Everything changed. Suddenly they were afraid of God and no longer felt like his children. Their relationship was broken. They tried to hide and keep secrets from God, and prayer went down the tubes.

People began to think of prayer as a duty, something they had to do to keep from getting into trouble or to stop God from getting angry. They forgot about God's great love. They lost the relation-ship and focused on rules and formulas. They thought, *If I can just do it right, I'll get the answer I want.* Many people even stopped believing prayer would make a difference.

Rules, Not Relationship

It didn't take long for prayer to become something that had nothing to do with relationship with God. People began to treat prayer as a magic formula—if you said the right words, in the right way, at the right time, you could convince God or the "universe" to do something for you. They even developed

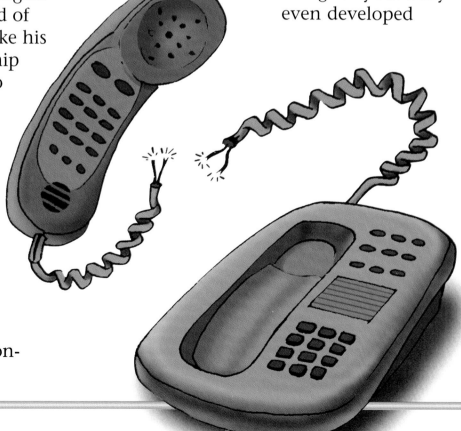

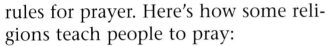

Some religions teach you to "pray" by concentrating on certain sounds and repeating them.

Prayer wheels like this are twirled to release the "mantras" or "prayers."

rules for prayer. Here's how some religions teach people to pray:

Rules Rule: You must pray so many times daily facing a certain direction. Rules tell you where your hands must be, when and what to do with your body—bow, kneel, sit, touch your head to the ground—where to put your feet and fingers, and what words to say for each position.

Words Rule: Certain words "magically" cause things to happen. Just repeat them.

Wheels Rule: Write prayers, or mantras, on paper scrolls. Attach them to wheels and turn them clockwise. This releases kind powers from the mantras and gains you merit or "goodness points." But, look out! Turning the prayer wheel counterclockwise can release bad powers.

You Rule: You're the only "god." Pray to yourself. It's silly to think there's anyone to help.

False Gods Rule: There are all kinds of gods. Some are even people who lived great lives. Use the right words, and they'll act or take your cause to a more important god.

Notice something? None of these "rules" see God as lovingly interested in us. Instead, they say we have to convince him to do something for us against his will. And there's no guarantee he'll do what we ask or even listen to us!

Our Misunderstandings

We might have some of these wrong understandings of prayer. Recognize any of these?

- We repeat the same prayers without thinking about what they mean.
- We must use the "right" words or phrases when talking to God.
- We don't need to pray. We can take care of ourselves, no problem.
- It doesn't matter whether we pray or not—it won't make a difference anyway. God isn't interested in us.

Built for Prayer

God's Design

Question: What exists in the remotest parts of Earth, the smallest town and the biggest city? Answer: Prayer of some kind and respect for God or gods! Why do people believe in God or a "god" and try all sorts of things to communicate with him? Because the desire to pray is built into us.

Any good car has one purpose—to move people around safely and comfortably. Every part of the car—wheels, battery, seats, wipers, transmission—is designed to fulfill that purpose.

Like a car, we're designed for a purpose—to have a relationship with God as our Father. All the parts God built into us—like thoughts, brains, feelings—work toward that purpose. They're all designed to help us communicate naturally with our heavenly Father. It's no wonder prayer is everywhere: It's the key to God's purpose for us!

In fact, it's not just we who are designed for prayer: *Life* works by prayer. God wants us to have the best possible life. That comes out of relationship with him—letting him care for, teach, and protect us—which happens through prayer. Want a great life? Pray!

One of a Kind

You're different from anyone who's ever lived! God had a one-of-a-kind design when he made you. That means you relate to God differently than anyone else does.

Every parent loves all their children. But each child has a different relationship with his or her parents. You like lots of hugs; your sister may not. You may enjoy playing ball with your dad; your brother may prefer doing something else.

It's the same with God. We each relate to him in a way perfectly suited to who we are. God has unique relationships with everyone he made. He loves us all equally. He has a special you-shaped spot in his heart. That means everyone has to develop his or her own relationship with God. Every relationship will be different, but they're all built by spending time with God. What will yours be like?

All Ears

God hears every prayer. He's not limited to one set of ears. He can concentrate on zillions of people at once while holding the universe together with his little finger!

These days computers "multitask" and run several programs at once. A computer sends a shuttle into space, directs its course, regulates oxygen, keeps instruments going, adjusts fuel usage, records astronauts' body temperatures, and much more. All at once! If people can make something that amazing, just think what God can do! He can hear the prayers of every single person at the same time. There's no way you or your prayers could ever get lost or missed. Not only can God hear everyone, he gives each of us his complete, loving, undivided attention.

God is all ears. He's listening to *you!*

God made everyone different. He has one-of-a-kind relationships with each of us.

Did You Know?*

- 88 percent of Americans pray
- 78 percent say prayer is important in daily life
- 63 percent pray often (25 percent pray sometimes)
- 65 percent believe they've had prayers answered specifically
- 79 percent say prayer can speed up recovery from sickness
- 86 percent of teens say they should pray more

*Summary report provided for Lightwave Publishing by the Roper Center, University of Connecticut (Storrs, Conn.), 1997. The report cited findings from the Princeton Survey Research Associates for the Pew Research Center, June 1996 and for the Times-Mirror Company, July 1994; the CBS/*New York Times* Poll, September 1995; Yankelovich Partners Survey for *Time* and Cable News Network, January 1995 and June 1996. Also, "Youthviews," Volume 3, Number 8, April 1995, The George H. Gallup International Institute, Princeton, N. J.

God's Will

Smart Living

With a new video game, the manufacturer's instructions say: "Do not sit on. Do not put in toaster. Do not use in water." Obvious! A video game works best when it's used for what it's made for.

Life is like that. God is not being mean when he tells us to do certain things (be honest, obey our parents, don't steal). He made us, and he made life. He knows how it all works best. These rules are his "manufacturer's instructions" for how life was made to work.

Doing things God's way is just smart living. It makes a fantastic life possible. God gave us an instruction manual (the Bible) to go with our lives so we would

know his way. It's easy to obey God when we know that everything he tells us to do is meant to help us have a wonderful life. His will is great! And it's written in the Bible.

Praying for Success

What's God's will got to do with prayer? Everything! Successful praying *is* praying God's will. It's successful because, if God tells us to do something, he'll help us do it. And if he says he'll do something, he will. The Bible says God's will is for us to be honest, be kind, tell people about Jesus, and so on. When we pray for these things, we can trust God to take care of them. The more we agree with God's written will, the Bible, the more he answers our prayers.

The key is to ask for what God wants to give, because we trust his love and know his way is best. Simple.

The Bible doesn't give God's will for everything, such as whether we should try out for the play. When we're not sure about God's will, we can still pray for it. Consider these prayers: "Dear God, my friends are in the play. I want to be in it too. Please make sure I get a role. Amen." Or: "Dear God, my friends are in the play. I'd like to join them. If it's what you want for me, please help me get a role. If not, I know that you know best. In Jesus' name, amen."

Which of these prays for God's will? The second! It makes sense to ask God to answer our prayers his way, not ours. We can pray without fear because we know God loves us. We can trust him to give us what's best.

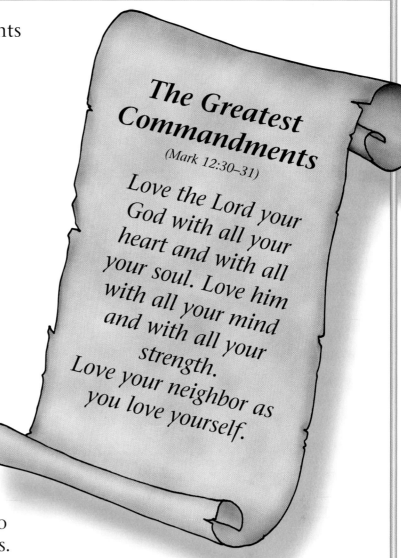

The Greatest Commandments
(Mark 12:30–31)

Love the Lord your God with all your heart and with all your soul. Love him with all your mind and with all your strength. Love your neighbor as you love yourself.

Cosmic Shopping Channel?

Want list: Best friend. Good grades. New jacket. My own room.

Some people pray as if God is a galactic superstore or a huge, cosmic shopping channel. How well do you know the people on the shopping channels? You don't! That's the problem with treating prayer like a shopping list. The whole reason for prayer is *relationship*.

God isn't a shopping network—he's a person. He wants us to know him, realize his love for us, and ask for things in that context. God enjoys giving good gifts. But he also wants to hear how we feel and what we're thinking. He wants to give us wisdom and help us grow. Why? We're his children! He's our Father. Talk to him from your heart. His answer will be fantastic!

What to Pray

Talk Types

"Guess what happened today!"

"You look great!" "I hope I make the team!" These are all examples of "pleasure" talk. This talk expresses who we are and what's going on in our lives. It's about the daily things that make life interesting and fun. With it, we get to know each other and express our love for each other.

"Did you make your bed?" "I need help with math." "Who's driving?" "Oops! I forgot the garbage!" These are "business" talk things. They have more to do with the nitty-gritty of daily living: chores, schedules, studies, and so on. With this talk, we help everyone do their part and find out who's doing what.

Both talk types are important.

Pleasure Prayers

Like "pleasure" talk, pleasure prayers are about relationship. We tell God how we're doing, what's going on, our hopes and dreams, and our wishes and fears. We take the time to let God in on our lives. And we take time to get to know him.

Pleasure prayers might be:

Family: Thanks for the great time tonight! Please give us a good holiday.

School: Help me do my best in the drama tryouts. Science class was fun today.

Me: I had a great day! Thanks for helping me tell the truth.

Friends: Sarah's very sad—please help her. I'm sorry I hurt Jon's feelings. Please forgive me.

Business Prayers

We need to "talk business" with God too. The Bible tells us to pray for certain things like our leaders, the church, and people who don't know God. God wants us to grow and learn to love others. Part of that involves praying for other people. So we need to take time to pray about the business of Christian living. In these prayers, we agree with God about the things important to him. These are more structured prayers and might be similar each time.

Some business prayers might be:

Family: Please protect our family. Help Mom and Dad make good decisions. Help us get along.

School: Give Miss Wilson wisdom to teach science well. Help Janey know you.

Church: Help Pastor Dan as he preaches. Show us good ways to help people in our community.

Country: Help our political leaders make wise decisions. Keep the police and firefighters safe as they do their jobs.

World: Please keep our missionaries, the Browns, safe and help them tell people about you. Please feed the people who are hungry.

Friends: Help Sandy and I get along. Thanks for helping John get better.

Me: Help me obey you. Please help me understand what I read in the Bible.

Find the following prayer situations in the puzzle below:

- Pray for those who hurt you (Matthew 5:44).
- Pray for workers in the harvest (Matthew 9:38).
- Pray that you won't sin (Matthew 26:41).
- Pray others will do right (2 Corinthians 13:7).
- Pray for God's people (Ephesians 6:18).
- Pray for open doors for God's message (Colossians 4:3).
- Pray for those in authority (1 Timothy 2:1–2).
- Never stop praying (1 Thessalonians 5:17).
- Give thanks no matter what (1 Thessalonians 5:18).
- Pray when in trouble. Sing praises when happy (James 5:13).

Types of Prayers

A Prayer Pattern

Any guesses who the best pray-er is? Jesus! Jesus loved to pray. Sometimes he even prayed all night! Jesus taught his followers about prayer. He even gave them a pattern prayer that teaches the key things to pray about. You probably know it. It's called "The Lord's Prayer" or "Our Father." Here's what it teaches:

Our Father in heaven: God has a loving Father **relationship** with us. We can relate to him as we do our human fathers.

May your name be honored: We honor God and what he's done. That means **thanking** him for how wonderful and loving he is to us.

May your kingdom come: God's kingdom comes by people getting to know him and obeying him. We pray for God's **church to grow** strong and healthy and for people to become Christians.

May what you want to happen be done on earth as it's done in heaven: We tell God we want his will. We pray **leaders** will have **wisdom** and want God's will.

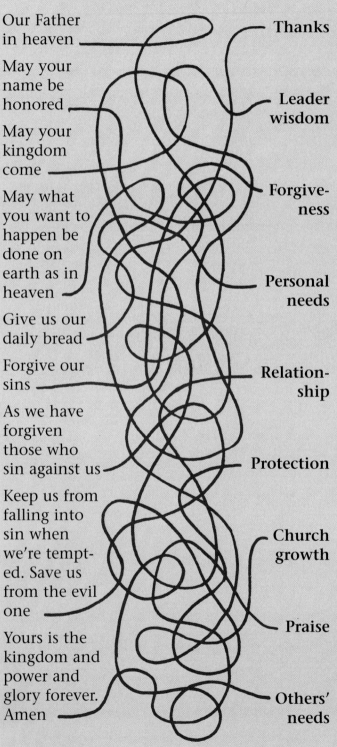

Match the phrase with the kind of prayer it is.

Our Father in heaven

May your name be honored

May your kingdom come

May what you want to happen be done on earth as in heaven

Give us our daily bread

Forgive our sins

As we have forgiven those who sin against us

Keep us from falling into sin when we're tempted. Save us from the evil one

Yours is the kingdom and power and glory forever. Amen

Thanks

Leader wisdom

Forgive-ness

Personal needs

Relation-ship

Protection

Church growth

Praise

Others' needs

Give us today our daily bread: We trust God to take care of us. We bring our **personal requests** and needs to him.

Forgive us our sins: None of us do God's will perfectly. So we ask God to **forgive** us and help us grow and become more like he wants us to be.

Just as we also have forgiven those who sin against us: Other people make mistakes. We need to forgive them when they hurt us and pray for **their needs** too.

Keep us from falling into sin when we are tempted. Save us from the evil one: We ask for God's **protection** from bad things and temptations. We ask him to help us choose the right way.

For yours is the kingdom and the power and the glory forever. Amen: We **praise** God because he has the power to answer all these prayers. "Amen" means we know God hears us and answers our prayers.

Public Prayers

Prayer isn't just for our private or family life. Praying with others is important! The church is people (each with a special relationship with God) gathered together to focus on God and his kingdom. Part of doing that is worshiping, praying, and singing together. In *worship* we tell God how wonderful he is. We invite him to work in the church, telling him we want to obey and love him more.

And we pray together. This public prayer is about the needs of the group and God's will being done in the world. When someone is praying out loud, we listen quietly and agree with the prayer. Jesus said, "Suppose two of you on earth agree about anything you ask for. My Father in heaven will do it for you. Where two or three people meet together in my name, I am there with them" (Matthew 18:19–20).

When Do We Pray?

In the Middle of Living

When you hang out with your best friend, when do you talk? Whenever you think of something to say! Think of God as your best friend. You can "hang out" with him all the time. Whenever you think of something to say or ask, go for it!

But let's get specific:

During:	You Might Pray:
Waking up	Thanks for good dreams. Help me be kind today.
Breakfast	Thanks for looking after me and giving me good food.
School	Help me remember what I studied. Bless Miss Jones.
Recess	Thanks for Sandy and for fun! Help John be kind.
Lunch	Please help this food give me energy for sports.
Going home	Help Mr. George drive carefully.
Sports	Please help me learn to dribble. Give Coach Hardy wisdom.
Dinner	Thanks for my great family and Dad's good cooking.
Trouble	Joey got hurt today. Please help him.
Night	What a great day! Thanks. Please give me good dreams.

Get it? Pray anytime, anywhere, about anything—right in the middle of living!

Set-Aside Times

Sometimes special needs come up: your mom has an interview, your sister is sick, or your friend wants to be a Christian. These are great times to pray.

We have other times set aside specifically to spend with God—church, family devotions, Sunday school, or bedtime. These are special times designed to focus on God and communicate with him.

Alone Times

You enjoy being alone with your best friend. That's when you talk about what's important to you and really get to know each other. It's the same with God. When you're alone with him, you can tell him your innermost feelings, what you like about yourself, and what you want help changing. You can tell him your secret dreams and wishes and ask him about his. Start setting aside five to ten minutes. As you get used to it, increase your time. Soon you'll be having such a good time with your Friend that a half hour passes in a flash! Alone times with God are the special times where you learn to understand his love. It's a great idea to have your Bible handy. When you read it before or after praying, God can use it to teach you and show you what he's like.

You can't grow a close friendship with someone you see once in a while or only when others are around. And you can't grow a close relationship with God if you talk to him occasionally or only at church. He wants a personal, one-of-a-kind friendship with you. That means only you and he can build it!

For Good Private Prayer Times

Choose a time when:
- You're wide awake. (The middle of the night's out!)
- You've done your homework and chores. (Prayer is no excuse to skip chores.)
- You'll have uninterrupted time. (Two minutes before ball practice won't do.)
- There's enough light to read your Bible by. (Although flashlight reading can be fun.)
- No one's going to bother you. (After the first breakfast call is bad timing.)
- There are no distractions. (No TV or music blaring.)
- You're comfortable. (Hanging from monkey bars gets distracting.)

How and Where to Pray

Say It with Your Body

Moses stood. David danced. Solomon raised his hands. Elijah put his head between his knees. Daniel knelt. They were all praying! Our bodies express our feelings. People know we're sad or happy by how we stand or sit. We use our bodies in prayer too. We hold or raise hands, bow our heads, close our eyes. . . . The key is to match our body to our attitude—and be honest about our feelings.

When we're . . .	We might . . .
happy	do a "David" and jump up and down, thanking God
sorry	lay face down
agreeing with others	stand with them or hold their hands
praying intently	kneel or sit with our head bowed
just talking with God	sit in our favorite chair

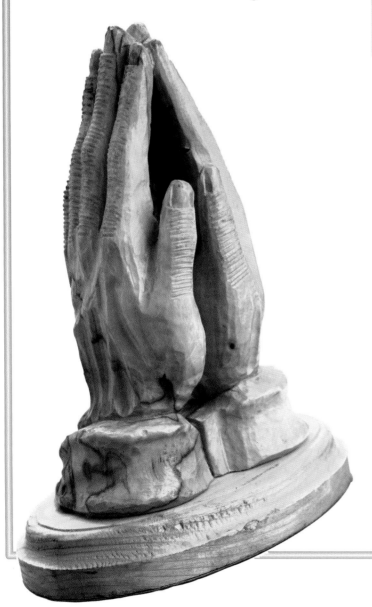

Say It with Your Tone

The words we choose and how we say them are important too. God loves us. And he is *God*: holy, pure, powerful. So we should pray respectfully. That means being polite, honest, and open. God deserves our honesty and respect. We can tell God how we feel, even if it's negative. But that doesn't mean shouting or being rude if we're angry. No way! We can say how we feel respectfully.

Say It with Others

Listen: You know those times when someone talks about one thing while another talks about something else, and neither listens to the other?

Frustrating! We need to pay attention to what people are saying.

Praying with others is like that. When one person is praying, everyone else should listen. Praying with others means we're saying, "Yes, please answer this prayer." And remember, public prayers are about things that matter to the whole group.

Mean it: Think of singing in church. We don't sing just to make pretty sounds. We're singing and praying to God! We should be paying attention to the words and thinking about their meaning.

Practice: Mealtime prayers at home are a safe place to practice public praying and to learn to pray in front of others. Ask your parents if you can take turns saying the blessing or "grace."

Say It in the "Closet"

Small, dark space. Clothes tickling your cheek. Shoes underfoot. Oh, and an old tennis racket for a seat. Closet prayer! That's not exactly what Jesus had in mind when he told people to go into their closet to pray. He meant, "Don't show off by letting everyone know you're praying." Prayer is about God and us, not about impressing people with how spiritual we are. That's why Jesus told us to pray in private.

Anywhere is a good place to pray!

There's another good reason for praying in a private place: Concentration! When we talk to someone, we look at their face and eyes. It helps us concentrate on what they're saying and see their reaction to what we say. God isn't with us in a body; he's spirit. He is completely present wherever we are, but we can't see spirit with our physical eyes. So we need to focus on him with our hearts and thoughts. To do this properly, it's best to close our eyes to get rid of physical distractions. As we get to know God through prayer, we'll "see" and "hear" him with our hearts.

Memorized Prayers

Borrow the Right Words

"I pledge allegiance to the flag of the United States of America, and to the republic for which it stands, one nation under God, indivisible, with liberty and justice for all." United States citizens learn these words by heart. They don't have to hunt for words for their promise. Long ago someone carefully chose just the right ones. Thinking about those words tells us what's important to the United States.

Sometimes we can't find the right words for our prayers. How should I pray for God's will? What's the best way to ask God to look after me? How can I pray for my friends to know God's love? When we run into trouble finding the right words, we can "borrow" prayers from others. Some people are good at finding great words for their needs and requests. We can make their prayers our own.

Owned and Unowned Prayers

You probably use memorized prayers already: the Lord's Prayer, "grace" at meals, bedtime prayers like "Now I lay me. . . ." The key is to think about the words you're using as you pray and about the person you're talking to: God! When you focus on the meaning of the words and speak sincerely to God, you make the memorized prayer your own. You're no longer "borrowing" someone else's prayer—you're praying from your heart.

Saying the words without meaning them just wastes words! It's like saying, "That meal was great!" every time you talk to your mom. Are you really talking to her? No, the conversation is meaningless. Memorized prayers work well for the right situations, when we own them and mean them. Otherwise they too become meaningless, unowned prayers.

Choosing Prayers

To make borrowed prayers your own, you'll want to find ones that you like, that mean a lot to you, and that express what you feel or need. Here are some places to look:

- Check out the prayer books some churches use.

- Your parents or friends might have favorite prayers they can teach you.

- Take time to write out your own special prayer—when you've got it just right, memorize and use it.

- One of the best places to look is the Bible. It's chock-full of fantastic prayers—especially in the Psalms. One example is Psalm 23, "The Shepherd's Psalm."

And remember, prayer is about relationship. You have favorite sayings or phrases you use with close friends. Used at the right times, they're fun. But letting them become the main part of your conversation gets pretty silly. The same with prayer. Our relationship is built by speaking from our hearts, telling God how we're doing, what's going on. And that changes from day to day. So should our prayers.

In the Bible, David wrote songs to God. You can borrow his Psalms for your prayers.

Using Scripture to Pray

You can pray Bible verses from memory. Or you can read the verses and go through them one phrase at a time, thinking about each line. What does it mean to you? Is there something you should respond to? What does it say about God? Pray that phrase, adding your own thoughts.

Try using these verses:
When you're worried: John 14:1
When you're afraid: Psalm 23:4
When you've done wrong: 1 John 1:9
When you want something: Psalm 37:4
When you want to praise God:
  Psalm 100:1–2

God's Answers

Yes: When Jonah ran from God, a big fish swallowed him. He prayed for forgiveness. God said, "Yes!" The fish spit Jonah onto dry land.

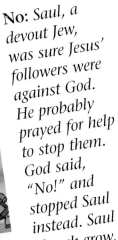

No: Saul, a devout Jew, was sure Jesus' followers were against God. He probably prayed for help to stop them. God said, "No!" and stopped Saul instead. Saul became Paul. He helped God's church grow.

Maybe or Wait: Joseph's brothers sold him as a slave. He probably begged God for help. But God said, "Wait." Much later, God made Joseph the second highest ruler in Egypt! Joseph told his brothers, "You planned to harm me. But God planned it for good!" (Genesis 50:20).

Preset Answers

Asking to borrow the car when you're twelve always gets a "No" answer. But "Can I do my homework?" gets a "Yes!" "Can I go to Sandy's?" isn't as clear. What's the difference? The first two have preset answers. The third doesn't. Prayers are like that.

"No" Prayers: The Bible tells us what God is like. It's clear God won't do some things. For example, God is love. Asking him for revenge on Jason won't work. Nor will asking to pass exams without studying. The Bible tells us to love our neighbor and to work hard. God won't answer prayers that go against what he says in the Bible.

"Yes" Prayers: Some prayers definitely get a "Yes." They agree with the Bible and who God is, or ask for something God said he'd do. For example, God said he'd provide our needs. So when we pray for them, we know he'll say, "Yes!" When God tells us to do something, he helps us do it. So praying for help to forgive a friend gets a "Yes." These answers are preset! We need to ask and trust God, but when we do, he does what we ask.

"Maybe" or "Wait" Prayers: Then there are the question marks—prayers the Bible doesn't cover, specific requests like "Please help me make the team" or "Please give me a bike for my birthday." The key is to pray for God's will. Then, whatever the answer, it will be best. We can trust God's love. Sometimes God answers, "Wait." Just like our parents won't let us drive before we have a license, God won't give us what we ask for when we're not ready. "Yes" might harm us.

Remember, we know that God hears *every* prayer. He always answers according to the Bible and what's best for us.

Parenting Answers

God also answers as a parent. The foundation of our relationship with him is being his children. We become God's children when we believe he sent Jesus to die for our sins.

Like our parents, God works to grow our character so we'll have a good life. If we disobey, do our parents talk football? Nope. They talk obedience. If we're fighting, do they take us to the mall? Not likely! They deal with the issue. In the same way, if we're disobeying God or fighting and not forgiving, God works on that. He wants us to obey him and forgive and love everyone like he does. Everything is on hold to deal with that. Then God moves on to deal with our other prayers.

Faith Stories

Start a collection of stories about God's answers to your prayers. You could divide the pages of a notebook down the middle. Write the prayer on one side and the answer on the other. Or just write out the

Jesus prayed for God's will all the time.

whole story. You could also write down family prayers and answers. When answers come, celebrate with Prayer Answer Parties. Soon you'll have a collection of stories that will really encourage your faith!

Whatever answer God gives, it's the right one. We can trust him because he's trustworthy. We can have faith in God because he's faithful—he always does what he says. And remember, God's will for us is the best.

25

Testing Our Faith

Ready?

Scuba divers test their equipment. Teachers test our knowledge. Why? If the person (or object) isn't ready for the next step—diving or seventh grade—they'll fail. Failure can be discouraging or even dangerous (especially in deep water)!

When it seems like God is silent or saying no to something important, we might doubt and wonder if he hears us. "If he loves me why doesn't he . . .?" we ask. This could be a test. Whatever it *looks* like, one fact doesn't change: God loves us and does what is best for us. He can always be trusted!

Why the Silence?

God has good reasons for what he does—like growing us to be like Jesus. He could be silent because:

You have to grow into it: You're asking for something you aren't ready for, like playing in a competition before learning the skills.

It might hurt you: You don't understand what would happen if you got what you wanted. Being friends with that cool kid could lead to a bad attitude that hurts you and your family.

God has something better: God says no to making the soccer team so that you can go on an amazing trip.

You need to know where you're at: God stretches you so you can see what your faith is like. When it seems he's not listening, we're tempted to stop trusting. The result? Often the answer doesn't come. But if we keep believing, eventually the answer comes, and our faith grows. Each time we hang on to trust

Prayer Checklist

- Develop your relationship with God by talking to him every day, not just when you want something or have a problem.
- Line up your prayers with who God is. (Don't ask him to be mean!)
- Pray for things the Bible says to pray for.
- Don't pray for what the Bible says *not* to pray for.
- Pray for God to do things according to his will, not yours.
- How is your faith? If it's low, God can increase it (Ephesians 2:8).

- Be thankful. Praise and thanks are important parts of prayer.
- Keep praying. Don't give up. God is always working even when we can't see it.

Don't Forget:
- Sins can come between God and us. Confess any sins (be specific) and ask forgiveness.
- Forgive people who've hurt you. Ask God to help. He understands how much it hurts.

it gets easier—we remember all the times God came through. Tell God your doubts and questions. Ask for help to keep trusting. Remember, it's all about relationship with him.

The Bible Speaks

"You will face all kinds of trouble. When you do, think of it as pure joy. Your faith will be put to the test. You know that when that happens it will produce in you the strength to continue. The strength to keep going must be allowed to finish its work. Then you will be all you should be" (James 1:2–4).

Joseph faced troubles when his brothers sold him.

"We are full of joy even when we suffer. We know that our suffering gives us the strength to go on. The strength to go on produces character. Character produces hope. And hope will never let us down" (Romans 5:3–5).

27

Listening to God

Walkie-Talkie Prayer

"James, this is Bond. I'm in position. Over." *Sssst.*

"Roger, Bond. Go on 'three.' Over and out!" *Sssst.*

That's walkie-talkie talk. Only one person can talk at a time. You say "over" to tell the other person it's his turn. "Over and out" means you've finished your conversation—kind of like "Amen" at the end of a prayer.

We don't say, "Over," when we pray, but maybe we should! It would remind us to stop talking and *listen.* After all, conversation is a two-way thing.

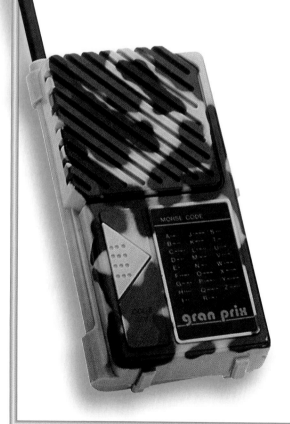

It takes at least two people, and each person should have a chance to respond. That means we have to stop talking. We can't listen while we talk. We can't get to know someone without listening.

We give God a chance to respond by waiting quietly in his presence. "Be still and know that I am God" (Psalm 46:10). God doesn't speak like we do, so how do we hear him? When we're quiet before God, new thoughts, understanding, wisdom, faith, or even God's peace might come. These things help us understand God's will better.

God Speaks in Many Ways

- *The Bible:* God helps us understand a passage or remember a verse that relates to our prayer. We listen by reading, studying, and memorizing God's Word.
- *Pastors and Christian leaders:* They've studied the Bible and spent time getting to know God. God can give them wisdom to help us. We should listen to them.
- *Parents:* God made our parents responsible for us. He gives them everything they need to help us grow into the people he wants. We need to respect and listen to them.

- *Older, wiser Christian friends:* Our friends can pray for us, give us advice, and help us find answers. If their lives show they're following God, their advice is probably good.
- *Life events:* God works everything together for our good. Sometimes, by paying attention to our circumstances, we can learn what God wants for us.
- *Strange events:* In the Bible, God used miracles, visions, dreams, and angels to talk to people! God can speak to us in dozens of ways!

In fact, God can speak anytime, anywhere, in any way he wants. Most of the time, though, he speaks in our hearts and lives in a way that doesn't seem like he's talking at all. But he is. Let's be quiet, ask God to teach us and give us wisdom, read the Bible, and listen every day. We'll find our thoughts going in God's direction—and that's the best for us.

George Washington Carver

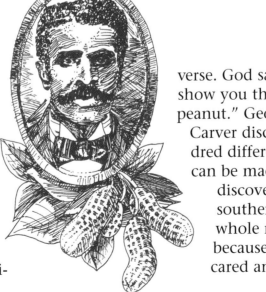

As a boy, George prayed for a knife to whittle with. He dreamed of one stuck in a watermelon out in the field. The next day when he looked, there it was! George learned that God hears and answers prayers.

Later, George became a scientist and asked God to show him the wonders of the universe. God said, "No. But I'll show you the wonders of the peanut." George Washington Carver discovered three hundred different products that can be made from peanuts! His discoveries helped the southern states build a whole new economy. All because he believed God cared and answered!

Working with God

Q **When we're bad, can we still pray?**

A A person can pray at any time for any need. When people do bad things or make mistakes, they need God more than at any other time. When we do something wrong, we need to talk with God about it and admit our wrong. We need to ask him to forgive us and help us learn and grow so that we can do better next time.

God knows we aren't perfect. He wants to give us wisdom and help us change. If we wait until we're good enough to pray, we'll never pray.

Q **Why do we have to pray when God already knows what we're going to pray?**

A We could never tell God something he doesn't already know. When we pray, we talk to God about the things God and we are doing together. God designed the universe to work a certain way, and prayer is part of his plan. Remember that one of the most important reasons for praying is for the person *praying* to be changed. So when we pray, we find ourselves becoming more of the kind of people that God wants us to be. *We* learn something from *God!*

Also, God wants to have a relationship with us. You wouldn't say,

"Why do I need to talk to my parents? They know what I need already." Asking God to meet our needs is one small part of prayer.

THANK YOU FOR YOU KNOW WHAT AND FORGIVE ME FOR SCARING YOU KNOW WHO WITH A FROG AND...

Q If God has it all planned, can we really change his plan by praying for things?

A No one can see how their prayers affect God. We know God is in control. We also know God hears and cares about our prayers and answers them. God could take care of everything without our prayers, but prayer is his plan.

God wants his people to be coworkers with him in this world. We work with him. Part of that involves prayer. Our prayers are part of the way God's work will get done. The Bible tells us repeatedly that our prayers make a difference.

Nothing takes God by surprise. He knows everything, even the future. Also, remember the main reason for praying—to get to know God better and let him teach and care for us.

Q How does God answer our prayers?

A In many ways. God is all-powerful. He can use anything he wants to work out his plans. One of the ways he answers prayer is by using other people. For example, God often uses doctors to bring healing. He uses generous Christians to give money to people in need, in answer to their prayers.

God will often give us wisdom and teach us in order to answer prayer. We may ask for more money. God may answer by helping us learn how to use what we have more carefully. Sometimes God uses angels to do miracles or intervene in some invisible way. He also uses processes and natural forces of nature.

And almost always, God changes our hearts when we pray. He works inside us to make us more like Christ in the way we think, talk, and behave.

Adapted from *107 Questions Children Ask About Prayer*, Tyndale House Publishers Inc., 1998. Used by permission.

Payoff!

Okay, you're praying. You're getting to know God and growing more like Jesus. What now? This is where it all comes together. God built us for prayer. Life works by prayer. Prayer brings the payoff—a great life!

Think—what you *really* want probably includes friends, a great family, fun, happiness, being loved and accepted, feeling safe, having your needs met, and doing what you love—what God created you to do. God has given us the ability to know and learn from him so our lives can be the best. Prayer makes it happen. Oh, not all at once. At first prayer may not seem like everything we've said. But if you keep praying, it will.

God knows how to do life well! And he loves giving good gifts. That means he enjoys doing things for us and helping us grow. When we know this without doubt, prayer becomes exciting and wonderful. The result? We want to pray more, which shows us God's love more, which gets us even more excited about praying!

A good prayer life teaches us God is love. He always:
- accepts, listens to, and wants to be with us
- helps in tough times, is there for us—is available
- believes in, trusts, and challenges us—gives us responsibility knowing we can do it
- forgives, corrects, and guides us—keeps us on track for his awesome plan
- laughs and cries with us—accepts our emotions
- provides for our needs
- shares his joy of life with us

What more could we want? Growing in prayer is growing with God. Growing with God is growing in life. God and his love never change. We can count on him!